Contents

All four partners of Architect Five, Junichi Kawamura, Hidetsugu Horikoshi, Takeo Matsuoka, and Hirotaka Kidosaki, worked in my office over a period of some ten years, where they took part in various projects and accumulated careers in and outside of Japan.

I was somewhat surprised when I first heard that they were going to establish themselves as a team, when each of them has more than sufficient ability and capability to make it on his own, and I have been observing their activities with great interest.

Today, looking at the 12 years since the establishment of Architect Five, it seems to me, the things they acquired in my office are undoubtedly reflected in their works, as well as in their strong dynamics as a team.

I truly believe their accomplishments would not be possible without their firm commitment towards Architecture, along with their devotion and enthusiasm for design.

I am looking forward to the future activities of Architect Five with anticipation, and hope they will be uncompromising pioneers in the world of Architecture in the 21st century.

Kenzo Tange

Architecture as Sensuous Comfort

by Maurizio Vitta

Architect Five's architecture is transcended by the principles on which it is grounded. At least according to what the architects themselves have said, the team is projected beyond architecture: it draws its design inspiration from the kind of moral tension and intellectual turmoil which we ought now to be used to when dealing with Japanese architecture, but which invariable manages to surprise us in some unexpected way. As always in cases like this, the only way of really describing the architecture is to talk about something else, in the knowledge that this "other thing" will be the most direct way of approaching the real issue.

In the beginning there is a number - the "five" that appears in the name Architect Five Partners but which does not refer, as we might at first think, to the number of architects in the team. As they themselves tell us: "People often ask us if there are five of us, but the "five" does not refer to the number of architects. It actually has multiple meanings". Architect Five's design philosophy is just as deeply grounded in magic and symbolic force as in mathematics and science, drawing on a tradition which is still as alive as ever in both the East and West and which uses numbers to organise, gauge, and balance everything, a sort of ineffable, ancient code in a world in which indeterminacy is gaining the upper hand. The "five" in Architect Five is something more than just a quantity: in actual fact it refers to the complexity of the grounding principles behind its architecture, tracing out a sort of conceptual map of its limits and prospects - in a word

it distinguishes if from the space and time of architecture.

There is nothing esoteric about all this. As we know, numbers are just a neutral configuration of a multiple system of meanings. They allude to quantities, but these quantities are just disembodied pure arithmetical values - silent, indistinct and dull - until they are brought to life and injected with meaning by the objects and concepts they refer to. This is where the symbolic process really begins, eventually even penetrating into the uncertain realms of myth, without breaking its tightly-knit bonds with the real world.

The Architect Five teams always begins its process of architectural design with the individuals and community expected to live in the space they create. "The architecture we design is founded on the down-to-earth perspective of the people who will use the structure. With all due respect to architecture as a means of artistic expression, we feel that architects are socially responsible for creating something useful to society". This statement expresses the team's professional credo focusing on: the social purpose of architecture. But such social commitment soon turns into a business approach embodying the firm's professional identity. As the architects themselves have pointed out: "It is this attitude that has enabled us to form a partnership and challenge new possibilities beyond the conventional framework in which big architectural offices take charge of most large-scale works and studio offices design private". This means that the Architect Five team is striving to get directly involved in the social dialectic, using its own

approach to design and construction to achieve this goal. This practical, feasible vision of architecture takes us back to the underlying principle behind the number "five". According to Architect Five the important thing about this phase in the history of mankind is dialogue among people or between human beings and nature. In light of this, the role of architecture and cities is to create room in our lives for such dialogues to take place. In other words, they are seeking to design comfortable, pleasant space. This is an acceptable but rather generic approach. It would be hard to find an architect who would not go along with this, at least in words. So what makes the Architect Five firm stand out from the rest? Well, first of all that number "five", which actually grounds their architectural design around three (another number with great implications) basic concepts, or in other words sensorial experience, awareness, and balance.

The body takes pride of place as the focus of sensorial and aesthetic interaction with the world, the main interface between the subjective world of the Ego and objective world of the Other. Architect Five uses the body as a means of getting back to primeval experience that takes sensation - the *five* senses - as providing both perceptual and cognitive access to everything. They point out that scientific and technological progress may have made our lives easier, but the deepest aspects of human life have changed very little over our 4000-5000 year history. It is because we have retained our natural instinct that we feel threatened by environmental pollution and destruction on both a local and global scale. Our five senses remain the same no matter how much our surroundings change. That means everybody has something in common - our five senses - on which to build the dialogue the team refers to. Bodily existence outside history is the element architecture draws on to mediate between the individual and nature.

Secondly, there is individual time, not time as it flows through life, but that moment of primitive innocence during childhood up to the age of *five*, the age when our experience of the world is still shot through with creative amazement and everything takes on vague, shifting outlines in our imagination, without being filtered and defined by the rigid schemes of rational thought imposed by education. This is the point at which the magic of the number five springs up in Architect Five's concept of design. It is treated as an arcane formula in which the intrinsic complexity of things is synthesised and structured. "Ever since ancient times", so the architects tell us, "the number five has denoted a special meaning in Buddhism and China. For example, according to the ancient concept of *Ying-yang wu xing shuo*, a combination *of ying-yang* theory and *wu xing shuo* - based on the *five* elements wood, fire, earth, gold, and water - was used to explain all things in life including the universe. Indeed, the figure "five" has been used since olden days to express a state of stability or perfect balance in reference to space or time".

These programmatic interpretations of the number "five" clearly project towards the deepest roots of existence in search of those origins lying beyond time and history in a primeval dimension immersed in myth and poetry or instantly evoked in our everyday experience. The Garden of Eden, where Adam went round naming every living thing and object, underpins a line of Western philosophical thought whose origins lie in the very distant past and which Giambattista Vico drew on in founding modern aesthetics back in the XVIIIth century. Vico identified in the "imaginary logic" of those primitive innocent "giants" populating the childhood world a "poetic logic" on which the rational thought of human civilisation is entirely based. The idea that the true nature of things can only be understood through language and hence only expressed in the form of metaphor was the kernel of a line of thought that made imagination the driving force behind knowledge, the matrix of thinking itself. Childhood innocence guaranteed a more penetrating form of reason capable of moving beyond computational rationality to grasp the vital essence of the world and track down truth at the utmost limits of the thinkable.

In the late XIXth century an Italian poet, Giovanni Pascoli, saw in "youth" - the epitome of the poet - those "who inhabit the shades of ghosts and the heavens of the gods"; during this same period Friederich Nietzsche expressed his admiration for the way Greeks were "superficial - *in their profundity*".

But Ancient Greece philosophy pricisely searched for the ultimate reason for everything in the primitive elements of the world; and the four elements that Democritus took to be the constituents of the world - water, air, earth, and fire - are roughly mirrored in the five elements of Oriental philosophy that the Architect Five firm draws on. Of course an important difference needs to be pointed out: according to Western culture, they are mobile, dynamic components determining the changing nature of the phenomena in which they combine in all kinds of new relations; in Eastern culture they ensure stillness, stability and balance. Opposite poles of existence - on one hand, spatio-temporal motion blending together the same old ingredients to provide cognitive intelligence and transformational action; on the other, the permanence and careful balance between different things as a way of resolving conflicts and contradictions - defining two quite distant philosophical views. Nevertheless, the idea of a handful of irreducible elements holding the key to the entire universe fits in with a vision of a world governed by simplicity and naturalness.

The philosophical connotations of the number "five" clearly define the conceptual-methodological approach of Architect Five's architecture, in which a thrusting towards a principle of regeneration based around the body, naive innocence, serenity, and a stable balance between different things turns into a synthesis - or "symbiosis" to use an expression Japanese architecture is so fond of - of these two cultures, but it also what triggers off any new design. "Architecture as sensuous comfort" is the firm's motto, echoing the grounding principle of modern aesthetics, according to which sensuous knowledge leads to truth just as effectively as reason.

The problem is then to transfer these guidelines from the realms of pure intellectual speculation into actual architectural design, in order to pinpoint exactly where they intersect and intermingle. In the end, it is a matter of superimposing two ideas so that they confront each other and we can see where their paths meet and where they go their separate ways. Architect Five offers us a point from which we can attempt to make this comparison. They note that "People tend to see architecture structured in a distinctive style as being easier to understand or evaluate, but the architecture we have designed does not follow a set format or style". The important thing for Architect Five is the actual situation that the architect is expected to deal with: environmental conditions, requirements to be met, targets to reach, and functions to satisfy. "We believe a design created around this kind of objective analysis and discovery process could effectively serve its purpose". This might seem a purely pragmatic approach, typical of lots of architecture, particularly in the United States. But it recovers conceptual ground as the practical situation being investigated allows us to sense its true nature. The architects are quick to point out that "the real process of elucidation starts with detecting some sort of hidden order behind diversified, complicated conditions, and analysing it - a process that should naturally take us to the essence of "design"". There is no doubt, then, that reality as it appears to the architect - imposing, twisted, contradictory, and full of humour, feelings or, if you like, beauty - must be the only design guideline for architecture which is aware of its key role in human-social life; but it is also true that we need to discover its hidden rules in order to understand it properly - in a word, only "hidden order" can actually represent it, and the symbolic force of the number "five" can only be disclosed through analysis.

These are the premises in light of which we can probe into the architecture of Architect Five: circumnavigation around its form and structure, but also a head-spinning descent into the depths of its internal logic, against the background of a design philosophy that reverberates through the fuzzy edges of the ever-changing image of all the firm's work.

The various constructions look like self-contained stylistic blocks, like islands in an archipelago whose common identity is reinforced by the sea that separates and unites them. The huge structures and strict geometric forms of the Setagaya Business Square make it look more like a town-planning project than an architectural design; but the only way of grasping its true nature is to study the intricate patterns of its site plan, the way if breaks up into a series of functional episodes spread across the city fabric, redesigning it and designating it for different and more advanced uses. Everything closed up and concentrated solely in the realms of architecture in this project, opens up in Tottori Flower Park, where architecture acts as a simple filter between human experience and nature. As in the Setagaya Business Square, here again XXth century architecture is just hinted it, alluded to, and indirectly evoked. The precision of rationalism has been replaced by a crescendo of eco-technology; but the ring, the long glass corridor, and in particular the large dome following the path of the sun and passing seasons definitely evoke the utopian ideas of Fuller. After all, Architect Five makes no mystery of the debt it owes to the great twentieth-century masters, such as Frank Lloyd Wright, Alvar Aalto, Kenzo Tange, and Richard Rogers. Nevertheless, the most characteristic feature of Architect Five's work is a typically Japanese sense of light, transparency and, we might add, the precious fragility of structures. The architecture of the Osada Electric Factory, Sony Music Entertainment Office, Sannohe Town Hall, and System Solution Center Togochi - to mention just a few - is a combination of solid structures and open spaces. It does not shape space and light: on the contrary, it might be said that it is space and light that structure the buildings, compressing its forms and shaping its outlines. It is as if light were seen for what it really is for the first time - a way of "seeing" things in order to "understand them", in the same way the "youth" in Pascoli's poem "shrinks to see better and grows to admire things".

This is probably where we ought to look for that "hidden order", whose unveiling marks the starting point of Architect Five's design work. If this were indeed the case, then it should not be sought in the design idiom that these architectural structures express, but rather in the shadows, silences, and unsayable illuminations. This takes us to the cutting-edge of Architect Five, the tangent between architectural design and creative artistry. Of course these architects reject the irresponsible idea of mere artistic show (although they point out the importance of understanding the history of architecture through the relations between materials and plastic arts). But they also claim that their work is based on dialogue with people or with the natural environment, or, simply, intuition; adding that "some people may criticise our approach for being over-ambitious, lacking in logic or too heavily dependent on instinct, but we believe that is what works best for us". And these are the main features of artistic and, more generally, aesthetic experience; these are also the most direct means of achieving the sensorial experience, awareness, and balance that are the real keys to Architect Five's philosophy of design. This takes us back - bringing out the circular, spiralling nature of our analysis - to the image of the number "five": a complex, multiform figure, as we have seen, that brings into play reason and feeling, the mind and body, nature and artifice, and excludes both separation and the identity of opposites, letting their true nature emerge obliquely in the conflicting motion of its elements.Architect Five has achieved this by reducing architecture to mere "body": "naive" body, as can be seen from its simple (and hence in some way "childish") relations with light and space; but also a sensitive body busy collecting, rearranging and mixing the primitive elements of things in search of their meanings and that precarious balance controlling the uncertain way in

which they interweave. This means that architecture does not live the kind of life characterising glass, steel, plastics or chemical colours, it lives like its inhabitants with their warm, fragile bodies, their constant moving along floors and walls guided by light bursting in from the outside or lighting up inside by touching handles, switches, smooth/rough/ soft/hard surfaces, by the smell of grass and leaves flowing through the gaps opening up to dawn and dusk, experienced in the secrecy of silence or the allegorical force of relations, closed away in meditation or open to communication, allowing the four elements of Western alchemy or five elements of Oriental wisdom to arrange themselves in figures explaining everything, time, history, memories, the fullness of being and emptiness of nothingness, life and the dark opposite it carries within. This is perhaps that "hidden order" that Architect Five is searching for and which is concealed in any significant work of architecture. Hidden order that must constantly be evoked and designed, devised and constructed, so that architecture can share in human life and patiently mark our complicated history. The message is actually almost alarmingly simple; but it must be reassembled and communicated with every new building project, design and construction, so that its memory and original meaning are not lost. This is the day-to-day task of all architects; the difference being that Architect Five has incorporated it in its programme, turning it into a design philosophy, a way of creating architecture or sort of imperative norm.

Works

Ogawa Art Museum
Chiyoda-ku, Tokyo

Site
Chiyoda-ku, Tokyo
Main Use
Art Museum
Architect
Architect 5 Partnership
Total Floor Area
650(m²)
Completion Date
1987

The Ogawa Art Museum was designed to occupy the first floor of a seven-story building in Sanban-cho, Chiyoda-ku. The building owner lives on the sixth and seventh floors while tenant offices occupy the second through fifth floors. Since separate entrances for the owner and tenants had already been installed on the first floor, the basic challenge of Architect Five was to create deeply tranquil spaces using the remaining space. In an art museum, the sequence from exterior space to exhibition room, or between the exhibition rooms plays an important role for people who come to enjoy the art works.

Visitors to the museum first enter the quiet entrance hall in black granite stone, after which they are led through the dimly lit corridor with a low vault ceiling into a high-ceiling exhibition room. Art works are displayed in large, medium and small exhibition rooms and low-ceiling corridors that link the separate rooms, each with an independent character. The black granite border stone, which serves as a baseboard, emphasizes the independence and continuity of exhibition rooms.

The small exhibition room is dedicated to permanent exhibits by well-known artists such as Ryuzaburo Umehara, Sotaro Yasui, Shoji Komoda and Toshio Arimoto who died at a young age. This idea came from Sadao Ogawa, the owner of Yayoi Gallery in Ginza and client of this art museum. Mobile walls have been employed in the large and medium exhibition rooms to expand the diversity in the way art works are shown. Facilities are hidden from view by the white louver ceiling, which is used in all rooms for uniformity. Mobile walls are employed inside the glass showcases to completely conceal the opening for sending in the exhibits. The overall finish is based on achromatic colors, with bronze used as accents on the door, door knob and border of the vault ceiling. What appears like reserved design of Ogawa Art Museum is in fact an attempt to appeal to more primitive elements of human sensuality regarding the essence of architecture - for instance, "properties of materials," "dimensional proportion," and "light and shade" - without depending on superficial and abstract approaches we often see today.

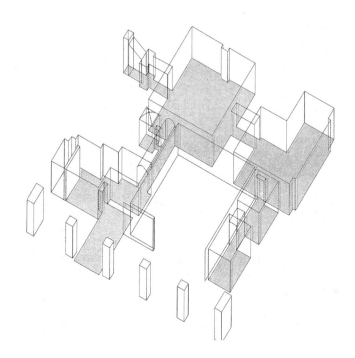

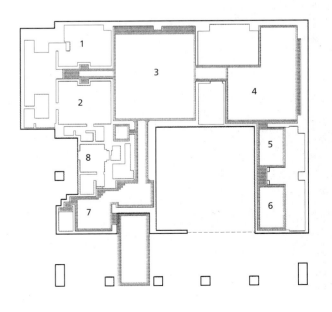

1 Library
2 Office
3 Exhibit 1
4 Exhibit 2
5 Exhibit 3
6 Exhibit 4
7 Entrance Hall
8 Storage

This page and
opposite top,
interior views
of the exhibition
space in sequence.
Facing page,
bottom,floor plan.

LINK dB-Soft Head Office / BUG Head Office
Sapporo, Hokkaido

Site
Sapporo, Hokkaido
Main Use
Office, Laboratory
Architect
Architect 5 Partnership
Structural Design
Umezawa Structural Engineers
Sculpture
by Isamu Noguchi
dB-soft BUG
Ground Area
9,699.00(m²)
7,099.00(m²)
Constructed Area
870.86(m²) 631.23(m²)
Total Floor Area
2,923.02(m²)
1,655.19(m²)
Completion Date
September 1988

"Link" is a general term referring to the architecture and landscape of two companies that specialize in the research and development of computer software. Located in Sapporo, Hokkaido, the site is designed to draw the blessings of nature from the surrounding pristine forest, and to withstand the harsh winter weather.

Two tennis courts straddle the border between the two companies' sites, and the sloping land around the tennis courts is left largely untouched except for the turfing.

The area around the courts is designed so that it can be turned into a stage for various events or even an amphitheater in addition to its original functions. The south-facing turf slope provides a delightful place in the sun for the audience to watch the events.

A semi-circular wall, aptly named "LINK," offers an aesthetic link between the two separate companies. The pristine forest outside the wall is left undisturbed as much as possible, while a well-manicured lawn stretches inside the wall. This is an attempt to reintroduce in the present day the traditional technique of shakkei, or using the natural scenery around the site, employed in the old architecture and gardens in Kyoto and Nara in Japan.

The plan takes advantage of the various natural elements of the site that make it such a special place. Occupants and visitors will be able to enjoy and touch the natural greenery, or come in contact with different levels of the undulating earth beneath. Work space surrounds the bright atrium filled with sunshine even in the darkest days of the harsh winter. The passive environmental conditioning plan incorporates geometric forms with small surface areas, carefully cut out picture windows and perfect outside insulation.

As part of environmental conditioning indoors, Architect Five employed T-joist beams in dB-SOFT's work space to create a column-free space, which also houses air conditioning and lighting for a more integrated approach.

For external facing, locally manufactured bricks are used for the fence and building base - parts that come in contact with the earth - as an expression of the companies' community-based spirit rooted in Sapporo. Vibration-polished stainless panels are used for the upper office portion as an embodiment of their vigorous activity in the high-tech area. The bricks and stainless panels have a hand-made texture, which cannot be found among mass-produced uniform materials, revealing an endless array of expressions in accordance with subtle changes in light. Architect Five expects the bricks and stainless steel to age beautifully over time.

Bronze sculptures by the sculptor Isamu Noguchi, who sympathized with and deeply understood the concept of the client and architects, are installed in the atriums of both dB-SOFT and BUG. Noguchi's work titled "Omphalos" sits in the middle of the BUG office, which is filled with the gentle sound of streams flowing down from a natural stone. It offers relief for our senses and overworked brain from computer work, inviting a deep sense of relaxation and comfort.

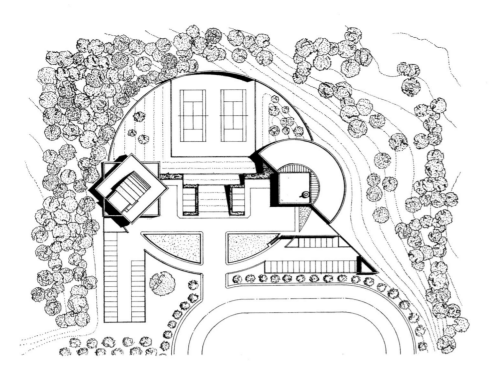

Site plan and
below, aerial view
of the building,
pristine forest
in the background.
BUG to the left,
and dB-SOFT
to the right.

Top, the lawn
and the tennis courts
linking the two
companies in one.
Bottom, the exterior
view of dB-SOFT
toward southwest.

Atriums offer
a moment of tranquility
in the office. Above left,
the sculpture,
"Omphalos" by Isamu
Noguchi in BUG.
Above right, atrium
in dB-SOFT.

Bottom, left to right,
1st of BUG Head Office,
dB-SOFT, and section.

1. Office
2. Meeting Room

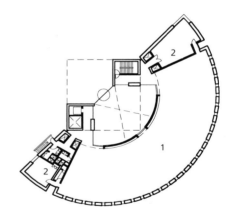

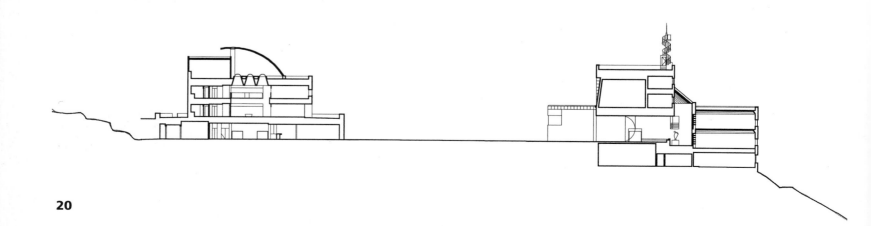

Morinaga Residence
Ota-ku, Tokyo

Site
Ota-ku, Tokyo

Main Use
Residence

Architect
Architect 5 Partnership

Structural Design
Umezawa Structural Engineers

Total Area
297(m²)

Completion Date
1988

The site is located in Den-en-chofu, an exclusive, green-filled neighborhood in Tokyo developed around a radial pattern. This three-story, two- generation household shares a common entrance.

The first floor is designed as a living quarter for the grandmother and aunt, the long-time residents of the house. It is planned around a big, south- facing living room that integrates with the garden, which serves to keep their ties with the times when the house was much older. Wood and Japanese paper are used in fittings, furniture and handrails -- parts that come in contact with the hand -- for the enjoyment of the feel of natural materials. It was not their original intention to use materials from traditional Japanese architecture: rather, Architect Five ended up with these materials when it looked for fine, native and more natural materials that fit nicely into the architecture.

The second floor has separate quarters for a spacious living room and private zone, demarcated by an open-ceiling staircase. The horizontal beam continues from the exterior eaves into the interior as part of the structure in the living room, dining room and bedroom. The partial low ceiling gives rise to a contrasting harmony with the high vault ceiling, creating a bright and calm space inside. Outside the house, the eaves and hood under the roof and balcony protect the walls and form shadows, adding to the diversity of view. On looking at the eaves and balcony that link the outside with inside, standing in front of the house one can almost feel how pleasant it would be to be in that room.

When Architect Five talks about housing, it does not believe in the need to use conceptual words or arguments, or techniques intended to draw attention. Instead, what it values most is that people feel good and enjoy living in the architecture it designs. To attain this, it pays particular attention to planning, materials, proportion and details.

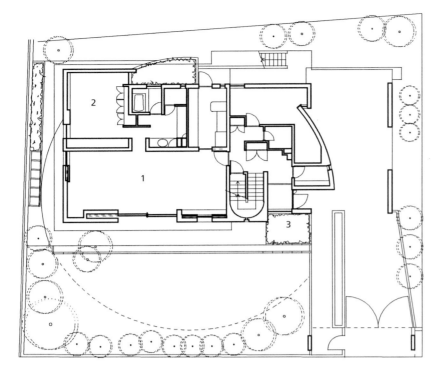

Ground-floor
and second floor plan,
and below,
the facade toward
the street.

1 Living Room
2 Bed Room
3 Entrance
4 Dining Room

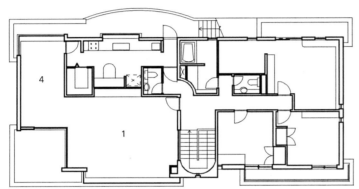

Interior view
of the living room,
under the concave
ceiling.

Setagaya Business Square
Setagaya-ku, Tokyo

Site
Setagaya-ku, Tokyo

Main Use
Office Complex/
Shops/Bus Terminal

Architect
Architect 5 Partnership

Associate
Tokyu Architect &
Engineers

Ground Area
21,328.96(m²)

Constructed Area
9,258.34(m²)

Total Floor Area
96,602.46(m²)

Completion Date
September 1993

The Setagaya Business Square project is made up of groups of high-rise buildings and medium/low-rise buildings. Contrary to the popular technique of structuring a project with a series of ten-story buildings, Architect Five intentionally concentrated a lot of bulk on the tower to secure open space at ground level and create a sound environment. The tower serves as a landmark for drivers going on to Tokyo along the Tomei Expressway. The side along the expressway has medium-rise buildings topped with a stair-like, green-covered roof floor, which steps down to the ground. Along the promenade on the north of the site stands a two-story restaurant. These buildings, surrounded by greenery, serve to conceal the expressway and create human-scale space.

The typical floor plan of the tower has a big impact on the spatial structure at ground level. In this project, the side core plan is employed to create wide-open spaces that offer an unobstructed view. The organization built on clear-cut axis offers an unbroken vista from one end to the other in all directions. This enables people to feel the site's vast expanse when they are inside and outside the building. Architect Five integrated the entrance space with exterior space, which is filled with greenery and water, creating urban spaces that comfort our senses. The project offers an astonishing diversity of elements. They include, for instance, the organization of space that comes in various types and scales, a variety of traffic lines that encourage people to stroll about naturally, composition of buildings from high-rise to low-rise buildings, and office spaces available in large, medium and small sizes.

The typical floor on the tower has cores inside the column tubes, which are located in the four corners, and a structural system based on long-span beam joists that produce a large, column-free space. Architect Five's idea is to install along the external wall "flexible" cores that let the sun in, and breathe in and out in the form of ventilation. It visualized workers hitting upon a good idea while moving from one place to another inside the building, taking a rest or refreshing themselves. To help support their inspirational activity, it tried to maximize the comfort level of core spaces, which provide "auxiliary" functions to the "main" office space.

The tower's silhouette is zigzagged at the corners and set back on the upper levels to minimize the impact of shades, wind and radio wave reflection. Architect Five designed the facade as an expression of functions of the interior space. In contrast to the center core plan, where windows occupy the entire external wall, various elements including the window, glass, stairs, and wall turn up in the side core plan. Subtle expression of these elements can be found in the pattern of external facing, which reminds one of lattice in traditional Japanese architecture.

Above left, skybridges
connecting
the buildings.
Above right, entrance
to the Yoga subway
station.
Left, exterior detail
of the mid-rise offices.

Right, floor plans.
Below, the open space
on the ground-level with
water and greenery.

1 Tower Square
2 Water Stone
3 Entrance Hall
4 Restaurant
5 Garden Court
6 Community Park
7 Bus Terminal
8 Stores
9 Office

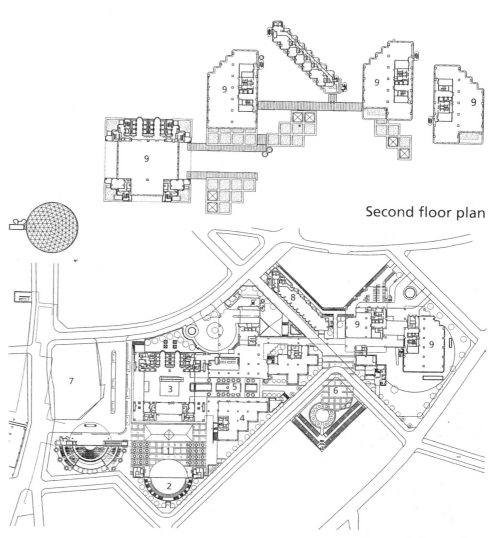

Second floor plan

Ground floor plan

Tower looking from
northwest at sunset.
The tower serves as
a landmark for drivers
coming into Tokyo along
the Tomei Expressway.

Moerenuma Park
Sapporo, Hokkaido

Site
Sapporo, Hokkaido

Main Use
Recreational Park

Master Plan
Isamu Noguchi

Supervision
Isamu Noguchi
Foundation

Architect
Architect 5 Partnership

Total Area
184ha

Completion Date
2004

"This place is crying out for form. And it is my mission to do just that," said Isamu Noguchi upon his visit to Moerenuma in March 1988, walking gleefully in the snow.

Moerenuma is one of the oxbow lakes produced by the meandering of Toyohira River that flows through the city of Sapporo. The 180 hectare-site including the lake had been a landfill area. At the time, Sapporo municipal government had a plan to include Moerenuma Park in its "Dream Green- Belt Plan," and had already launched the park area development while it continued to add to the landfills.

Isamu Noguchi insisted that the project be started all over again, saying, "we need to draw up a master plan that covers the whole area." He said he could not consent to undertake the park's design unless that condition was met. When Isamu learned the municipal government was reluctant to change parts of the plan in relation to state subsidy, he demanded the government to disclose all the pertinent conditions. After the conditions were sorted out, he accepted the restrictions, not to compromise, but as an opportunity to further deepen his unique thoughts toward the process of creation.

Isamu Noguchi then asked Architect Five to join the project as architects for the construction and completion of Moerenuma Park as they worked together in one of the previous projects. However, on December 30, 1988, just a month after the master plan was completed, Isamu Noguchi passed away in New York.

During his funeral, which was held just after New Year, discussions were held on what should be done about the Moerenuma Park project. The difficulty of completing the park, which itself could be seen as one huge sculpture, seemed overwhelming. Still, people who gathered there had a strong sense of

mission to bring the project to fruition -- they knew Isamu Noguchi had talked enthusiastically about his dream of creating this big park in Sapporo to many of his friends including those at the Isamu Noguchi Foundation in New York. With the understanding of and request by Nobuo Katsura, deputy mayor (current mayor) of Sapporo, the parties concerned confirmed that the project would continue. It was decided that Sadao Shoji from the Isamu Noguchi Foundation would join the project as supervisor, under whose guidance Architect Five would oversee the architectural design.

This park can be regarded as a culmination of all park projects handled by Isamu Noguchi. The Isamu Noguchi Foundation gave wholehearted support by presenting previous drawings and materials that might be of use in this project, and supervising the design. People concerned in the project including municipal government staff went to see the landscape works launched by Isamu around Japan and talked to workmen who took part in the creative process. Also, many Japanese architects including Takashi Sasaki, who have worked with Isamu Noguchi in the past, and Masataka Izumi of Mure, Kochi, extended their full support to this project.

Moerenuma Park was opened to the public in July 1998 after 60% of the project had been completed. The completion of "one big sculpture that teaches us about the relationship between nature and humans," a message Isamu Noguchi wanted to convey to the 21st century, is scheduled in 2004.

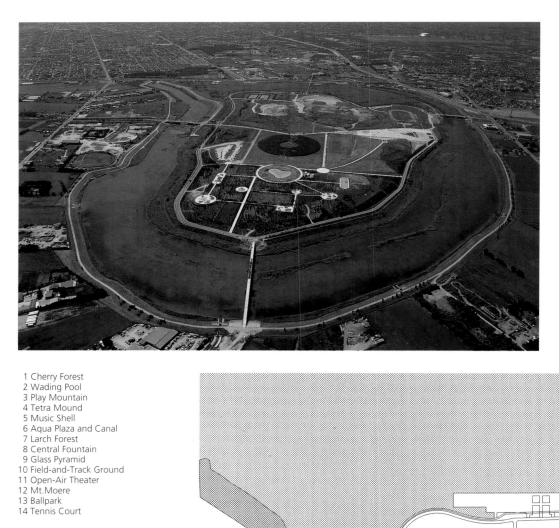

Left, aerial view of the
Moerenuma Park,
The site, formerly
a landfill,
was transformed into
the key park
in the Sapporo
Greenbelt project.
Below, master plan.
Facing page, Moere
Beach.

1 Cherry Forest
2 Wading Pool
3 Play Mountain
4 Tetra Mound
5 Music Shell
6 Aqua Plaza and Canal
7 Larch Forest
8 Central Fountain
9 Glass Pyramid
10 Field-and-Track Ground
11 Open-Air Theater
12 Mt.Moere
13 Ballpark
14 Tennis Court

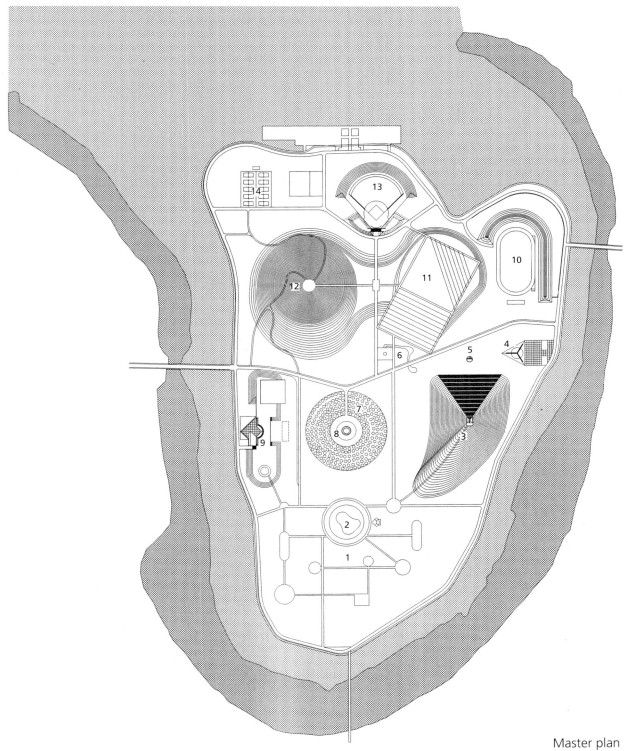

Master plan

Play lots, with colorful play equipments by Isamu Nogichi, are dispersed among the Cherry Forest.

Looking toward the top of the Play Mountain. Below, Slide Mountain.

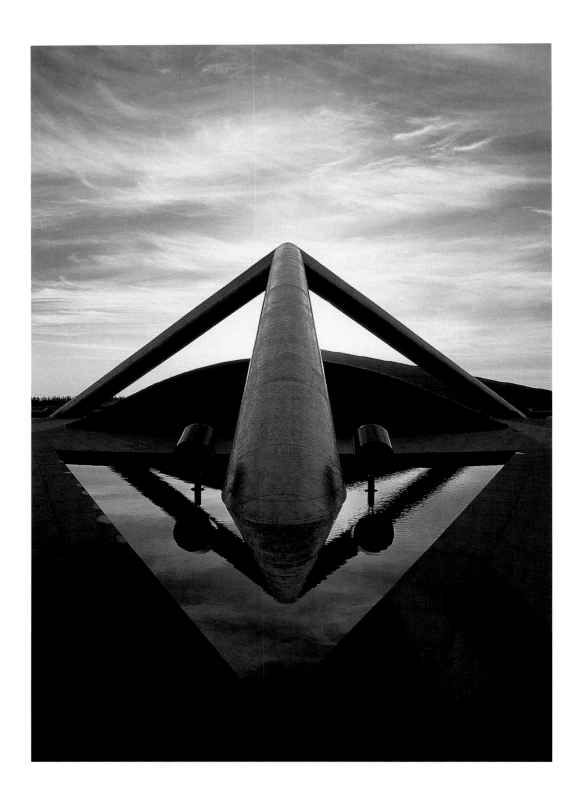

BASE
Midori-ku, Nagoya

Site
Midori-ku,Nagoya

Main Use
Factory,Laboratory

Architect
Architect 5 Partnership

Structural Design
Umezawa Structural
Engineers

E&M Design
ES Associates

Ground Area
14,336.81(m²)

Constructed Area
2,709.84(m²)

Total Floor Area
4,200.56(m²)

Completion Date
May 1992

The new challenge of Architect Five in designing this factory, which assembles and manufactures dental and medical equipment, was to incorporate the concept of hoigaku in accordance with the client's request. Hoigaku is a traditional science of judging one's fortune from directions. The combination of scientific architectural planning and hoigaku may sound odd to some, but it in fact has great significance in the way we treat space.

Since the ancient days, hoigaku, or feng sui in Chinese, has had significant, if subtle, impact on the life of Japanese people. However, most present day Japanese, even those who understand it in theory, would probably question the idea that building layout and planning are influenced by hoigaku. Still, it has survived to this day, perhaps because many of its teachings have proven to be reasonable and suited to the cultural climate of Japan. It may also have something to do with the national character. In the old days, people used divination as a technique for planning a project in certain places, which served as checkpoints to ensure the safety and soundness of construction. Similarly, Chinese feng sui examines the natural elements and invisible energy harbored by the site, and prescribes measures to remedy any flaws in the building or the site.

The power of divination and feng sui has been pushed into the background in cities and urbanized areas. Still, when we constantly strive to find what certain places or space mean to us, to draw the best out of that particular place, we are in fact playing the role of a fortune-teller. If our "reading" of the place is correct, the architecture built on the site breathes life, taking advantage of all the benefits the site can bring. If not, it creates a cold, inhuman atmosphere. One could perhaps interpret hoigaku and divination today as some form of warning, which tells us not to work against the natural order of things. In designing the architecture for this project, Architect Five studied the environment of people working in and out of the factory, surrounding conditions and local scenery by referring to hoigaku to make the most of the prospective factory site. As a result, an integrated, landscape-based plan was developed around the courtyard that links the two factories and the prospective factory site. Noise- and heat-insulated aluminum curtain walls in a circular arc line the building's Shinkansen side. The quieter side, which boasts cherry blossom trees and a pond, has cores that hold systematized equipment including EV and toilets, among which refreshment space is dotted. The two sides represent the contrasting concept of ying - yang, or movement and stillness.

The structural system used to secure a 25m span inside the factory plays an important role in brightening up the factory atmosphere. The laboratory and observatory have similar lens-shaped roofs ("UFO" roofs) that seem to float in the air - the distinctive features that symbolize the unique image of the factory. Architect Five named this project BASE in the hope that the architecture would take root in the earth and grow on the energy emitted by the site.

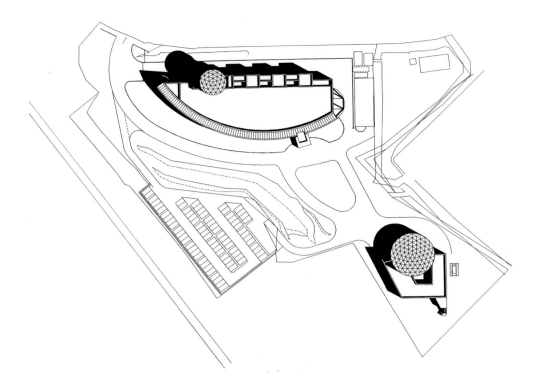

Left, overall view
of the factory
from south.
Below, exterior detail,
the combination of
aluminum panels and
glass on the
curved exterior.

Left, interior view of the factory. Below, from bottom to top, 2nd, 3rd, and 5th floor plan. Facing, cross section and, interior view of the lounge at the top.

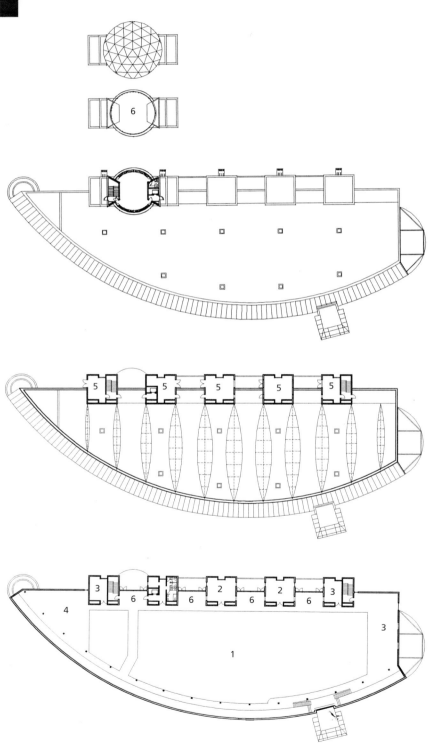

1 Factory
2 Office
3 Meeting Room
4 Central Laboratory
5 Machinery
6 Lounge

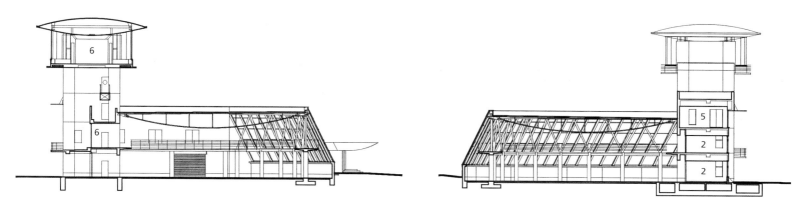

Plateau
Minami-tsuru-gun, Yamanashi

Site
Minami-tsuru-
gun,Yamanashi

Main Use
Cottage

Architect
Architect 5 Partnership

Structural Design
Umezawa Structural
Engineers

Total Area
1,552(m²)

Completion Date
1992

This rental villa, named Chalet de Plateau, enters the view of drivers after passing by the Lake Yamanaka and village office. The gently sloping site faces the path along Lake Yamanaka. It is subject to national park building code, which prescribes the rate of greenery and dictates that the building must be set back by five meters from the site boundary and 20 meters from the lakeside path.

The idea of Architect Five was to take advantage of these restrictions to preserve the view of the lake and Mount Fuji through the tall pine and Japanese maple trees growing on the setback area. Also, its challenge was to set aside a tennis court and parking to accommodate as many vehicles as possible for the rental villa. Architect Five decided that a collection of separate buildings rather than one big building would be better suited to the area.

A semi-underground parking was built on the side of the slope, and a tennis court above the parking. Ten separate villa units and common facilities are arranged around the tennis court. The architects linked the units with pilotis-like roof for the purpose of registering the structure as one building. The roof had the effect of creating a sense of unity as a village surrounding the plaza.

Independents units come in three types. The units along the bypath on the Mount Fuji side have pilotis: their bedrooms are located inside the semi-underground structure facing the courtyard, carved out along the site's slope.

The two units on the eastern side, large and small, combine into a large unit through the entrance. The tennis court serves as the village plaza. Surrounded by pilotis, each independent villa basks in the spectacular view of Lake Yamanaka and Mount Fuji as well as the refreshing breeze from the forest.

Architect Five has sought to maximize the benefits of the site's features in its architectural design, thereby creating spaces that please our senses.

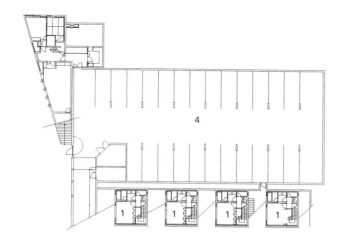

1 Cottage
2 Tennis Court
3 Entrance Hall
4 Parking

B1 floor plan   Ground floor plan

Facing page,
looking out to
the tennis courts
in the center.
This page, top,
from left to right,
1st and 2nd floor plan.
Above, interior view
of the cottage.

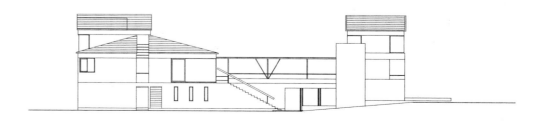

Dr. Shikata Residence
Isumi-gun, Chiba

Site
Isumi-gun, Chiba

Main Use
Residence

Architect
Architect 5 Partnership

Structural Design
Umezawa Structural Engineers

Ground Area
3,330.96(m²)

Constructed Area
380.86(m²)

Total Floor Area
283.30(m²)

Completion Date
November 1995

The project's overall frame is based on the image of a space that flows and pauses between the self-standing RC walls that enclose and open out into the surrounding forest, lush greenery on the east, and winds and view that pass from north to south. Carefully arranged among the existing trees, the flexible space is enveloped by a big roof that follows the gentle curve of the undulating site. The subtle and delicate gaps between the roof and floor plan produce a pleasantly wide space that stretches deep inside. It represents a stream of space organization - and a source of sensuous joy - that characterizes Japan's traditional architecture, extending from the garden to the verandah, to the door and windows on the opening, to large rooms.

Fresh breezes from the lake pass through the trees in the south garden and make their way through the large north-south opening. To the north, two greenhouses placed around the courtyard block the northerly wind while opening up views beyond the structure.

One of most important challenges was to generate a cozy environment in a space that has a huge air volume, created by the big opening and grand roof. Instead of using conventional air conditioning, which produces air currents and noise given the size of the equipment required, Architects Five employed a radiant heat air conditioning system as an ideal environment adjustment device for this space.

The studio has pursued radiant heat air conditioning, which plays an important role in our environmental adjustment plans, as a means to produce a snug environment for people who will be spending most time in the house.

In this project, large areas of louver-shaped radiant devices were incorporated and the whole house was covered with external insulation materials so that the floor, wall and ceiling retain heat and function as radiators. The system has been designed as a mild environment adjustment device suited to the climate in Japan. In winter, the radiant heat device can be run continuously at low temperatures while in summer, the air is dehumidified by cold radiation and condensation in the radiator. Aesthetically, the see-through louvers demarcate space and organically integrate the structure, building service and architectural design to produce a relaxing space.

Located away from the cities and close to the sea, the house is designed to accommodate friends who often come to visit and party on weekends as an integral part of life here. Positioned between two walls that run north and south, the dining room looks out on the courtyard to the north, arranged back-to-back with the living room that opens out on the sunny garden to the south. The house is designed so that people in the house are able to move around freely through the kitchen that extends north to south, or other routes. The simple structure generates spaces and traffic lines that offer maximum diversity and flexibility for its occupants. To the east of these two walls, the breakfast room is placed between the master bedrooms, which command a fine view of the panorama over on the opposite bank, forming a private zone together with the studio. A Japanese-style room and entrance are placed on either side of the wall that runs east and west, forming a guest zone in the western portion of the house.

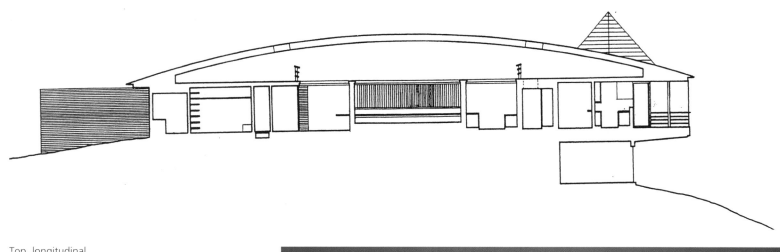

Top, longitudinal
section.
Right, facade to the
garden.
Below, site plan.

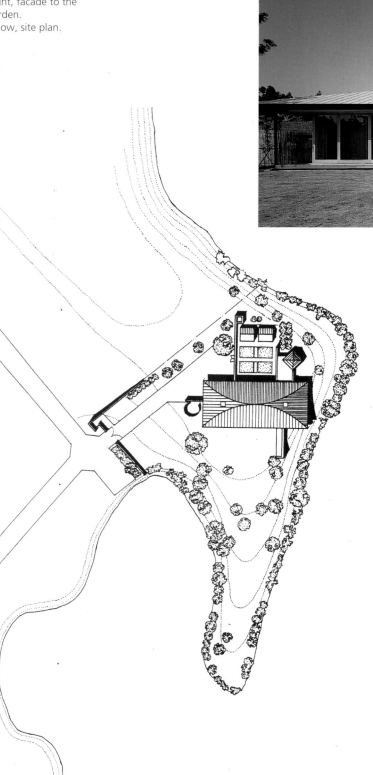

Top, Japanese-style verandah realizes the symbiotic relationship between the interior and exterior space. Below, looking out to the garden from "Tatami Room".

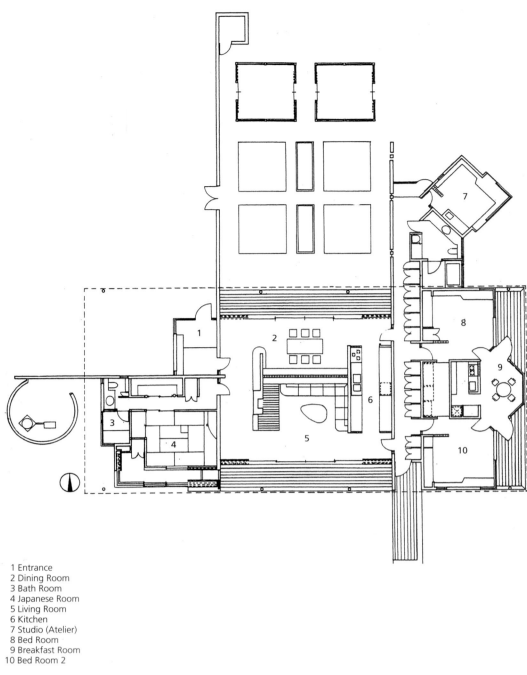

1 Entrance
2 Dining Room
3 Bath Room
4 Japanese Room
5 Living Room
6 Kitchen
7 Studio (Atelier)
8 Bed Room
9 Breakfast Room
10 Bed Room 2

Left, the living room air-conditioned by louver-shaped radiant heating devices. Below, the living room with doors fully open.

SSCT System Solution Center Tochigi
Shiotani-gun, Tochigi

Site
Shiotani-gun, Tochigi

Main Use
Computer Testing Center

Architect
Architect 5 Partnership

Structural Design
Umezawa Structural Engineers

Ground Area
17,729.87(m2)

Constructed Area
2,728.79(m2)

Total Floor Area
4,993.82(m2)

Completion Date
March 1995

"Inforest Tochigi", a next-generation high-tech park planned by Tochigi prefectural government, is located among the lush greenery of the Goryo Farm and plateau on the banks of Kinugawa (Kinu River). In our integrated master plan, which seeks to offer a sense of continuity, the whole area has been designed to give the feel of vast, uninterrupted fields. Various lots are placed around an organic-shaped park that holds water and greenery in the center. The lasting thing on our mind in this project was to draw up a checkerboard-like development plan found among many conventional industrial parks.

The project's central facility is the SSCT, or System Solution Center Tochigi, run by a third-sector organization developed by private businesses and national / prefectural governments. The SSCT is Japan's first facility dedicated to the testing of software and hardware as well as networks between personal computers and related equipment.

In the design of this project, Architect Five took pains to preserve the site's strikingly beautiful undulation and harmonize the project with the surrounding forest and rows of cheery trees. To achieve this effect, it designed the building so that it seems to "float" on the gentle slope while emphasizing the horizon to let it become part of the natural environment. Its main aim is to create a pleasant living space through the fusion of the original landscape and architecture.

The semi-underground area carved out of the slope serves as a portico for inconspicuous parking and service facilities. The first floor, which sits above the semi-underground level, is designed for column-free office space. The trussed structure - with fine members that interact aesthetically with trees in the background - serves to incorporate elements of dialogue with nature, a role played by the pent roof, eaves and verandah in traditional Japanese architecture. The column-free interior space measuring 22.4x 96 m offers the flexibility required to meet diversified needs for future testing.

By contrast, the second floor, where the area under the waved roof opens out into the wood-covered roof deck, provides free space for refreshment and relaxation.

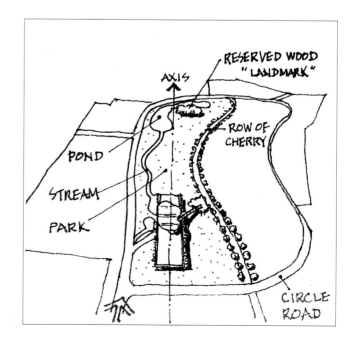

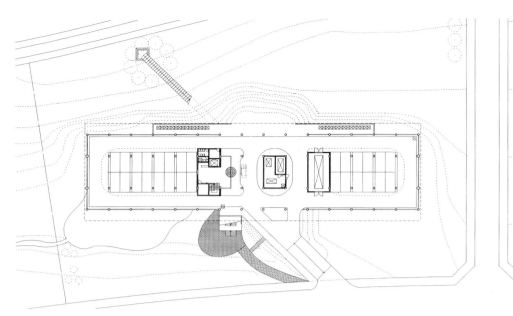

Left, site plan.
Right and below,
the facade of the
building is characterized
by two large horizontal
slab lines holded by
delicately designed
member trusses.

59

Left, the walkway connecting the upper terrace to the outside. Below, and oppsosite, the member trusses designed with close interaction with the surrounding environment.

Right, the first-floor refreshment level, contains restaurant and other reading-leisure facilities. With roof designed in free, curved forms, interior space tends to blend in with nature and has been built on-site using curved steel girders.

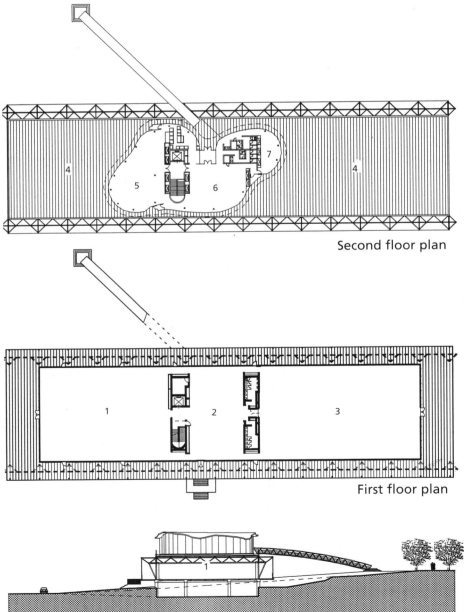

Second floor plan

First floor plan

1 Office
2 Entrance Hall
3 Testing Room
4 Wooden Terrace
5 Restaurant
6 Seminer Room
7 Relaxation Room

The second floor, under the waved roof opens out into the wood-covered roof deck, providing free space for refreshment and relaxation.

Sannohe Town Hall
Sannohe-gun, Aomori

Site
Sannohe-gun, Aomori

Main Use
Town Hall

Architect
Architect 5 Partnership

Structural Design
Umezawa Structural Engineers

Ground Area
3,115.61(m²)

Constructed Area
1,645.68(m²)

Total Floor Area
5,225.46(m²)

Completion Date
April 1996

While municipal governments in the surrounding area move into new buildings in the suburbs, Sannohe town with a population of 14,000 chose to rebuild on the same site. Residents of the Aomori town had hoped the newly designed architecture with its unique identity would help revitalize the downtown. In fact, the site occupies a pivotal position in the town's urban planning, where its historical, cultural and natural axis (mountains and rivers) intersect with the commercial axis along the prefectural road.

This town hall will be a new landmark to represent the Sannohe town. Architect Five believes that town hall architecture, as the town's symbol, should breathe new life into the consciousness of each citizen. There were days when people expected little more than administrative services from town halls. Town halls of the future, however, should be a place where citizens feel free to visit whenever they like, draw and exchange information or promote communication. All these considerations have been incorporated in the design of Sannohe Town Hall.

Since the site is accessible from three sides, Architect Five integrated promenades and a plaza into the plan and built roads that run through the site. Pass-through routes would lead visitors back to the commercial district and help rejuvenate the town. The office building, Health Center and assembly building are separate but linked by a huge wind shield room open to traffic 24 hours a day. The south-facing plaza, surrounded by a lobby with administrative service counters, stretches out into the open to produce a feel of expanse. It combines with the 20m-span of the town hall building, which continues into an open area, to secure a sense of oneness. To promote access by town residents, the assembly building is designed to accommodate lecture meetings, mini concerts, citizens' galleries or other events while the assembly is not in session.

It is the citizens who will shape the future of a town hall. Architect Five believes it helped them start on their track by providing the fundamental framework - or the space - to develop a huge range of possibilities.

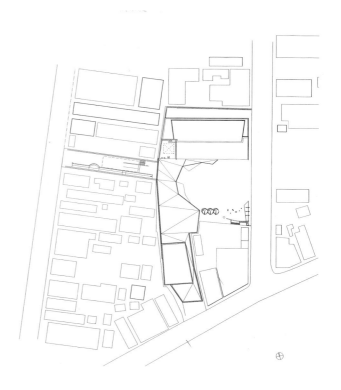

Left, interior
of the lobby and
the administrative
counters.
Below, the assembly
under the waved ceiling.
Bottom, floor plans.
Facing page, interior
view looking out
to the plaza.

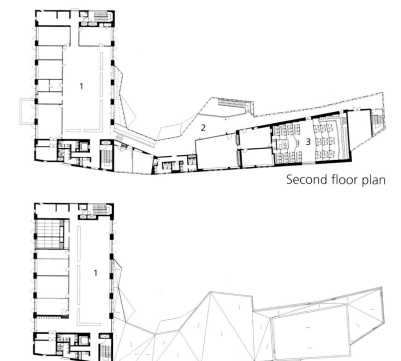

Second floor plan

1 Office
2 Lobby
3 Assembly Hall

Third floor plan

Left, cross section. Below, distant view toward the entrance of the Town Hall. Facing page, detail of the entrance composition.

Tottori Flower Park
Saihaku-gun, Tottori

Site
Saihaku-gun,Tottori
Main Use
Flower Park Complex
Architect
Architect 5 Partnership
Structural Design
Umezawa Structural Engineers
Total Area
14,500(m²)
Completion Date
April 1998

Located in Tottori in western Japan, this flower park project has been planned on a hilly area near Oyama-Iki National Park that looks out on the distant Sea of Japan. The project, based on the basic theme of "Geo Natural - Geometry of Nature," is designed to create spaces in which people are able to get in touch with nature, flowers in particular.

The hills with interlocking valleys on the site are left undisturbed and utilized to feature flowers and trees. By way of contrast, a flat, circular observation corridor measuring 320 meters in diameter is established at a certain height to be used as the main route for visitors. The corridor offers a wide range of sequences for encounters with nature in different places. For instance, you may look down on, rather than look up, a treetop, move through the branches, or climb down below ground level to see underground roots. When you reach a valley, you may find yourself looking out over the whole park and surrounding landscape from a height of 25 meters, or perhaps passing under a waterfall. In other words, visitors are able to observe flowers and trees from many new angles they have never experienced before.

Groups of flowers are planted in a geometrical layout according to season so that different shapes and flowers emerge each season. In the center of the circular corridor, a flower dome measuring 55 meters in diameter sits half buried in the ground. The dome is tilted 35 degrees, equivalent to the north latitude of the site, in accordance with the sun's orbit. This positioning enables visitors at the center of the dome to observe how the sun moves along the structurally designed orbit during the vernal and autumnal equinox as well as winter and summer solstice. Also, the north of central axis, which runs parallel to the earth's axis, faces the direction of the Polaris.

The "nodes" that embody different functions -- such as the entrance, exhibits, tropical greenhouse and restaurant --mark the four cardinal points around the circular corridor. Each of the node incorporates black (genbu), red (shujaku), blue (seiryu) or white (byakko), colors that were used to symbolize north, south, east and west in ancient Japanese cities, which had derived from urban planning based on Chinese feng sui.

The project combines geometrically organized architecture, founded on structural planning that sympathizes with the intrinsically rational nature of plants, with the ever-changing, unrestricted and complex elements of nature. It is an attempt to contrast and harmonize the two - to build a landscape of well-balanced symbiotic relationship between humans and the natural environment.

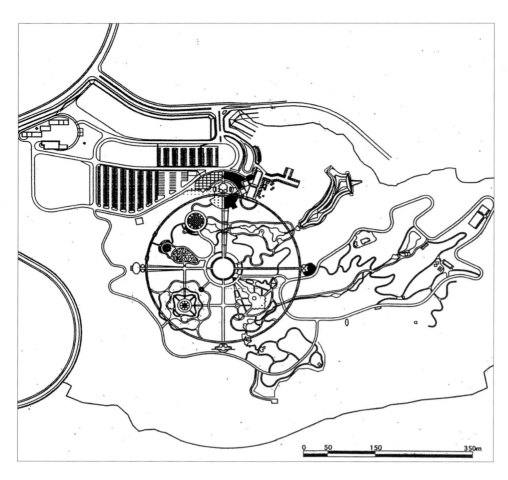

Left, site plan,and below,
model photo.
Facing page, corridor and
Flower Dome in the back.

0   50   150   350m

East

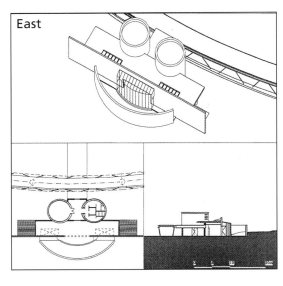

North

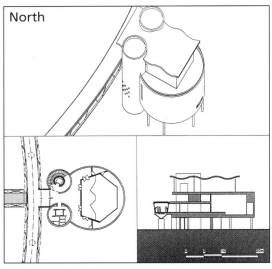

South

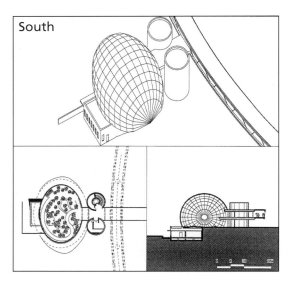

West

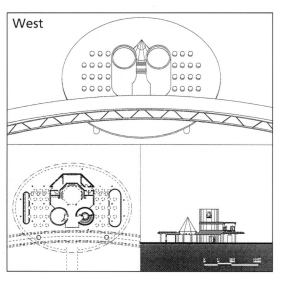

Left, axonometric, plan, and section of 4 "nodes" at cardinal points. Below, aerial view of the Flower Park, overlooking Mt.Daisen beyond.

Left, Flower Dome
elevation.
Bottom, the interior
of the skywalk.
Right, the skywalk
leading to the Flower
Dome at night.

Minami Ibaraki Tenno Housing
Ibaraki, Osaka

Site
Ibaraki, Osaka

Main Use
Housing

Architect
Architect 5 Partnership

Structural Design
Umezawa Structural Engineers

Total Area
27,897m²

Completion Date
1998

Architect Five's architectural design starts with looking at the project from the viewpoint of people who are going to actually live in the building. In this project, its aim has been to design a housing that protects the safety of occupants' living and offers a pleasant environment in which people can enjoy their life. While technological innovation, invention and sophisticated information technology have altered our lifestyle, we believe the yearning to get in touch with nature and beauty is intrinsic and universal because human senses have changed very little over time. It is important, therefore, that the "dwelling," in which we spend the most of our lives, should be able to respond to our basic quest for such sensuous fulfillment.

How can one create collective living spaces that will meet the needs of future lifestyles? To meet this challenge, Architect Five organized a professional design team comprising structural designers, building services engineers, planners, interior coordinators, landscape designers, artists and developers. Each member presented his or her opinion from residents' perspective and finally checked the process from a professional standpoint. As a result, the studio was able to design a collective housing in which various elements are in harmony with each other.

In Japan, building a home is considered a once-in-a-lifetime accomplishment for individual homeowners. A private house is built to last about 50 years at most, in contrast to the West where it is not uncommon to build houses that survive several generations. It is about time we reconsider the life cycle and asset value of a house, and how the two are interrelated. Many of the buildings that collapsed in the 1996 Hanshin Earthquake could have survived for many more years or decades had it not been for the disaster. In designing the Tenno Housing, Architect Five

was mindful to apply its lessons from the earthquake so that we would never have to experience a similar tragedy again. It is based on its belief that the most important factor that determines the asset value of a building lies in its earthquake resistance strength.

In this project, the primary concern is to protect lives and property, guarantee the building's durability in accordance with contemporary lifestyle, and offer collecting housing that would last a lifetime. Also, it has been intention of the studio to drive a wedge on the collective housing construction in Japan, which still is trapped by supply-side-oriented ways of thinking.

Morita Headquarters
Nagoya, Aichi

Site
Nagoya,Aichi
Main Use
Office
Architect
Architect 5 Partnership
Total Area
5,500(m²)
Completion Date
1998

For an architect, nothing is so precious as the opportunity to work with clients who have a deep understanding and enthusiasm for architectural design. The late Mr. Akio Morita, the renowned founder of SONY, was one of them. The Morita Headquaters Building, located in central Nagoya, became the first piece of work by Architect Five for the Morita family. The building exterior has been designed to resemble a sake brewery, reflecting the shop's 330-year history in the field of sake brewing.

A prominent feature of the Morita Head Office Building is the sky garden that dots the building. Some bulge out into the exterior space, while others are deeply inset above them or spread in a belt-like fashion. This technique of interspersing a building with plants creates a comfortable environment inside the building and adds lush greenery to the city: it suggests a viable and effective approach for the future office design.

In this garden, the tree roots are trimmed and trunks held in place by a tie rod to reduce soil pressure. The beam depth is cut as much as possible by the use of light soil, keeping the garden compact to minimize impact on office space on the lower floors. Also, the floor continues into the garden on the same level to offer a sense of continuity, oneness and comfort.

Sekiguchi Doll Garden
Ito, Shizuoka

Site
Ito,Sizuoka

Main Use
Museum

Architect
Architect 5 Partnership

Structural Design
Umezawa Structural
Engineers

M&E Design
ES Associates

Ground Area
14,087.44(m²)

Constructed Area
1,172.9(m²)

Total Floor Area
1,376.4(m²)

Completion Date
September 1998

The site is located on a slope in Izu Peninsula National Park. Dense forests cover the surrounding area, through which islands off Izu can be viewed on sunny days. Sekiguchi Doll Garden is a museum built by a doll manufacturer to celebrate its 80th anniversary. It houses a collection of western dolls from different genres.

In designing this museum, Architect Five tried to incorporate the natural landscape into the interior to enable visitors to view the dolls in a green environment full of natural lighting. Fragile dolls vulnerable to light are protected by way of space organization and method of exhibition. Since the exhibition space is arranged on sloping land, the floor level for a four-block section was lowered by 80 centimeters from block to block while maintaining the building height. It was designed so that changes in the spatial impression would alter the visitors' fame of mind to be prepared for a different set of dolls.

Stone veneered columns constitute the exterior wall.

The interval between the columns is covered either by glass, which takes in the exterior landscape, or insulating wall as means of protection for antique dolls vulnerable to light.

These two types of enclosures give different expressions to the building. Since the building faces south, the vertical rib columns, a main feature of the building, function as vertical louvers in summer. In winter, they produce long strips of light inside the building, reminding people the time of the day with the length of the shadows.

The building is constituted by simple elements: continuous gable roofs, vertical louvers that gently take the light in and variations in the spatial structure. Sekiguchi Doll Garden was designed to incorporate changes of the seasons to provide an

opportunity for visitors to enjoy the richness and comfort offered by this special place. We hope visitors will be able to feel the gentleness and warmth of dolls at this environment-based museum.

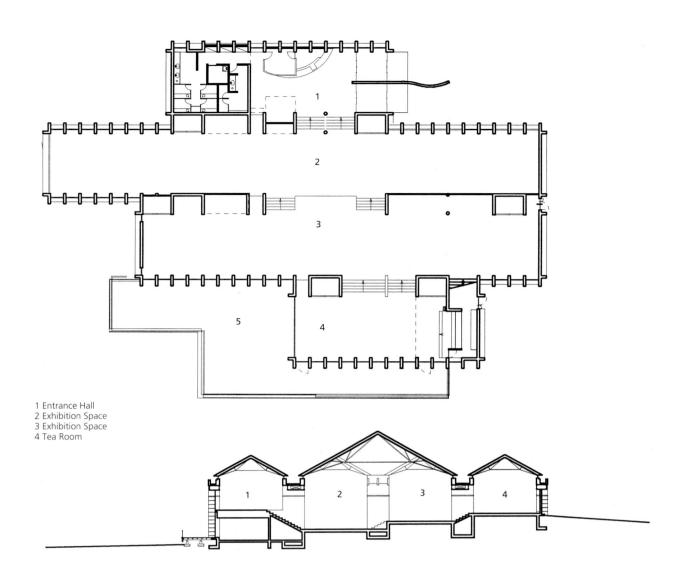

Left, floor plan.
Below the interior
of the exhibition space
articulated by
the subtle changes
in the floor levels.
Opposite page,
interior view
of the tea room.

1 Entrance Hall
2 Exhibition Space
3 Exhibition Space
4 Tea Room

FIVE
Shibuya-ku, Tokyo

Site
Shibuya-ku, Tokyo

Main Use
Studio Architect 5

Architect
Architect 5 Partnership

Structural Design
Umezawa Structural
Engineers

Ground Area
100.97(m²)

Constructed Area
79.16(m²)

Total Floor Area
462.59(m²)

Completion Date
December 1996

This small office building was designed to house the studio office of Architect Five. The studio believes that one of the keys to creating office spaces for people who actually work there would be to translate their feelings and sensuality into our own in the design process, as architects often do in designing their own houses. Based on its experience in designing several offices, Architect Five tried in this project to create working spaces in which people feel at home and architecture that pleases their senses. The process began with understanding the features of the site.

The site, which faces a wide road to the northeast, has a small frontage. The view of the greenery of Yoyogi Park and skyscrapers in Nishi-Shinjuku stretches to the north. The direct sunlight does not make its way into the building but the sun's rays from the north function as a steady light source as in an artist's studio. Creating a space with a big opening to take advantage of this panoramic view, therefore, became the central theme of this project. To make up for the small site area, and hence small typical floor area, a modest open-ceiling space was set aside on alternate floors. The open ceiling helps put together the space that tends to be broken down by the floor, and prevent communication gaps produced by the division. The panoramic view that spreads to the north and the gentle sunshine find their way into the building through gaskets and the simple, low-cost L-shaped corner window in wide flange shapes, which extends over two floors. The balcony and floor around the opening are set forward with cantilevers, creating a column-free, pressure-free space.

The balcony, which serves as a refreshment space, accommodates escape ladders, entry for fire brigades and an area for glass cleaning. By decking the balcony floor with wood, a sense of continuity with the wood flooring

into the room is obtained. Also, it enhances the sense of security when stepping on the wide opening. The balcony and large opening with open ceiling on alternate floors add a human dimension and sense of activity to the town. The elevators positioned on the south-facing side serve to reduce heat load of direct sunlight. The sunshine brightens up the utility room and exterior stairs and turns them into refreshing spaces. The aim of the design is to offer a setting in which occupants are able to feel the weather, passing of time or other changes during the day when they leave their desk and move to another place inside the office. Also, they can breathe in fresh air and feel closer to nature. The idea is to create a pleasant environment for occupants who will be spending most of time inside the building.

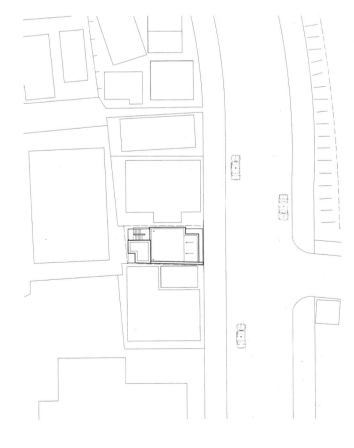

Left, the big opening introduces soft northern sunlight fully into partners' room on the top floor. Below, floor plan. Facing page, the atrium piercing two levels adds sense of openness and activates the communication among staffs.

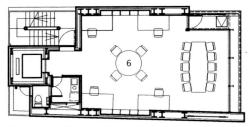

Seventh floor plan

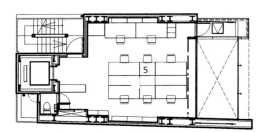

Sixth floor plan

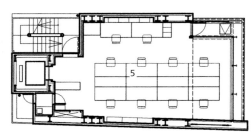

Fifth floor plan

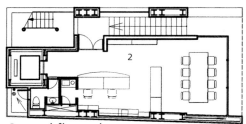

Second floor plan

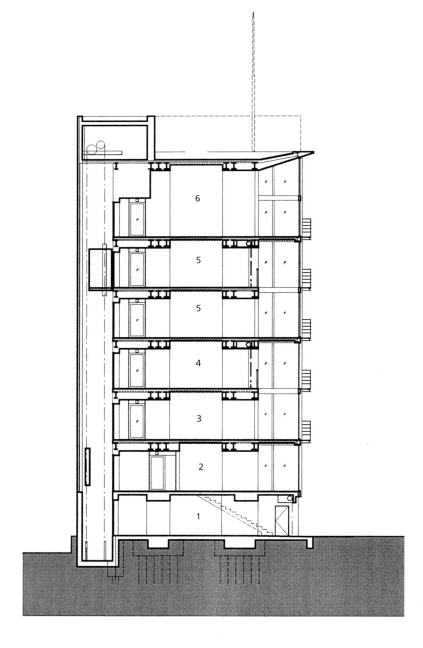

1 Parking
2 Reception, Meeting Room
3 Work Room
4 Library
5 Staff Room
6 Partner Room

Sony Music Entertainment Shiroganedai Office
Minato-ku, Tokyo

Site
Minato-ku,Tokyo

Main Use
Office

Architect
Architect 5 Partnership

Structural Design
Umezawa Structural
Engineers

M&E Engineers
ES Associates

Ground Area
2,243.25(m²)

Constructed Area
1,784.58(m²)

Total Floor Area
9,442.03(m²)

Completion Date
May 1998

Throughout their long years of history, Kyoto, Nara, Kurashiki and other age-old cities in Japan have managed to maintain a coordinated townscape even though houses were added or rebuilt along the architecture of the era. This may be attributed to an established code by which newcomers must abide in the form of hidden order, conventional practice and consideration for others.

In defining the boundary and road in this project, Architect Five adapted the ancient wisdom of using bamboo shades and green screens to block the view while letting the sunlight in to meet the needs of the new era. Translucent glass louvers, supported and suspended by stainless wires, define the smooth curve along the irregular-shaped site facing the road.

They also function as vertical louvers to alleviate sun's rays from the east. The rooftop garden, which came into being as a result of setback to meet the off-site shadow control, masks surrounding buildings from view. The green stair-like terrace conceals the opening from nearby buildings and serves to block the afternoon sun.

At the eye level, people passing by the road can see the spaces stretching inward from the large-span, high-ceiling pilotis entrance, which reminds them of the huge green expanse of the garden of the Institute for Nature Study that extends behind the site.

In all design processes, Architect Five places importance on the integration of architectural design, structure and building services - and flexible, versatile and generous space it produces. Almost all design-related efforts are dedicated to coordination works, or integration. The process is akin to a quest for harmony among various sounds and tones. We believe it is the wonderful music, and not the design of the musical instrument, that

moves people. To create an unrestricted atmosphere, Architect Five began by searching for ways to carve out a large, column-free, rectangular space from the irregular-shaped site, which faces the Institute for Nature Study. The odd-shaped area that remained is used as core space. The stairs, elevators, passage to WC and refreshment corners are located in naturally-lighted spaces facing the road so that people in the building could refresh themselves. These complicated functions are enveloped by a flexible drape in the same way as a wrapping cloth.

The structure and building services in the office zone, which is the main space, are exposed to secure ceiling height. This helps eliminate the sense of oppression one often feels in a large space with limited ceiling height. Diagonal grid beams, a natural selection on the L-shaped large-span office plan type, are used with regular sleeves for each beam. Supply and return ducts are placed on distributed arrangement in accordance with the structural grid.

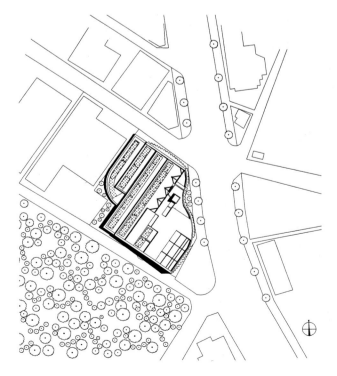

Top left and below, detail of the glass louvers suspended by stainless wires. Top right, undulating walls seen from inside. Bottom, floor plans.

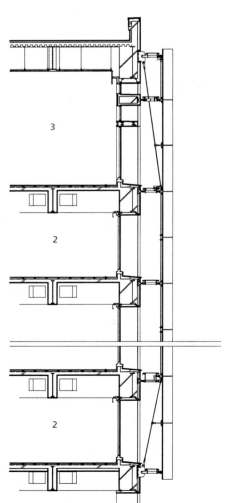

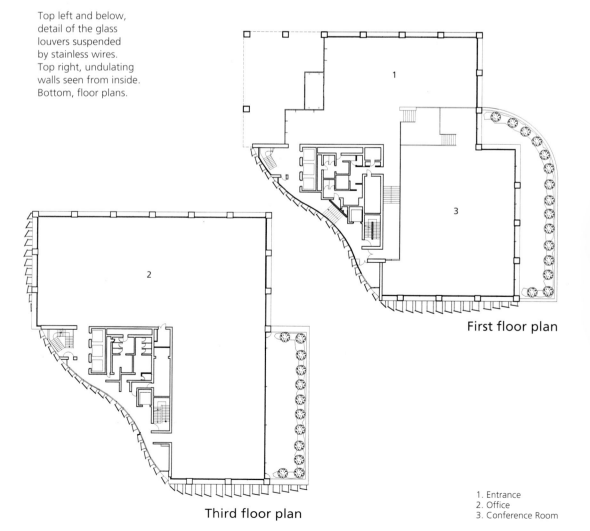

Third floor plan

First floor plan

1. Entrance
2. Office
3. Conference Room

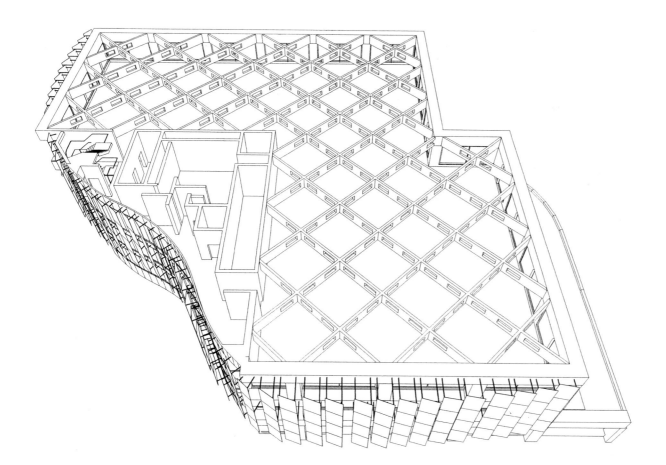

Top, axonometric.
Bottom, interior view
of the lobby, and its
diagonal beams.

Looking up
the glass louvers
on the street-side.

The building facade,
wrapped up
in the translucent
envelope of glass louver.

1 Entrance
2 Office
3 Conference Room

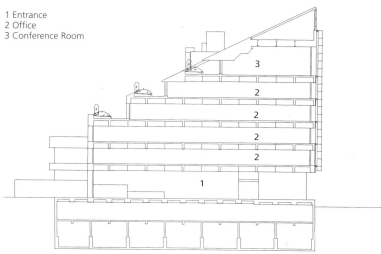

List of works

OGAWA ART MUSEUM
1986 - 1987 Tokyo

KUWAIT MOSQUE PROJECT
1986 Kuwait

KANDA UMEZAWA BUILDING
1986 - 1987 Tokyo

LINK / dB-SOFT HEADQUARTERS
1986 - 1988 Sapporo

LINK / BUG HEADQUARTERS
1986 - 1988 Sapporo

TURTLE COVE PROJECT
1986 Guam

HIMEJI GYMNASIUM PROPOSAL
1986 Hyogo

MATSUSHITA RESIDENCE
1986 - 1987 Tokyo

PARCO TERASAKI JEWELRY
1987 Tokyo

SPLINE
1987 - 1990 Tokyo

KOJOHAMA HOSPITAL PROJECT
1987 Hokkaido

INO HOSPITAL
1987 - 1989 Hyogo

KOHOKU NEW TOWN COOPERATIVE
HOUSE
1987 - 1989 Kanagawa

SUZUKI RESIDENCE
1987 - 1988 Tokyo

MORINAGA RESIDENCE
1987 - 1988 Tokyo

NISHIGATA RESIDENCE
1987 - 1989 Tokyo

SETAGAYA BUSINESS SQUARE
1987 - 1993 Tokyo
Associate: Tokyu Architect & Engineers

IZUMI INN PROJECT
1988 - 1990 Shizuoka

SAPPORO ART COLLEGE PROJECT
1988 - 1989 Sapporo

THE CLUB SHAKESPEARE
1988 - 1990 Hokkaido

MOERE NUMA PARK MASTER PLAN
1988 - Sapporo
Master Plan: Isamu Noguchi
Associate: Isamu Noguchi Foundation

SHINJUKU NISHIGUCHI BUILDING
1988 - 1991 Tokyo

MOI DAIKANYAMA BUILDING
1989 - 1991 Tokyo

HATAGAYA HAT HAUS
1989 - 1992 Tokyo

HAYASHIBARA BUILDING
1989 - 1993 Tokyo
Principal Architect: Richard Rogers

EXPO '90 / KALEIDOSCOPE
1989 Osaka

SEZON MUSEUM
1989 Tokyo

YAKUYAMA RESIDENCE
1989 - 1991 Tokyo

KURITA RESIDENCE
1989 - 1991 Tokyo

KOBAYASHI RESIDENCE
1989 - 1991 Tokyo

MOERE NUMA PARK/ GLASS PYRAMID
1988- Sapporo
Schematic Design by Isamu Noguchi

BASE/OSADA ELECTRIC FACTORY
1989 - 1992 Nagoya

HACHIOJI YOKAMACHI
REDEVELOPMENT
1989 - 1990 Tokyo

YAMANAKAKO HOUSE
1990 - 1992 Yamanashi

RAIKA SAPPORO PROJECT
1990 - 1991 Sapporo

OITA ASO RACING PARK/MACHINE
PLAZA ROYAL ROOM
1990 - 1992 Oita

OITA ASO RACING PARK/VIP HOTEL
1990 - 1992 Oita

WATANABE RESIDENCE
1990 - 1992 Tokyo

IKEGAMI APARTMENT
1991 - 1993 Tokyo

MIYAGASE DAM ARCHITECTURAL
PROPOSAL
1991 - 1992 Yamanashi

NIKKEI PRINT SUIDO BUILDING
PROJECT
1991 - 1992 Tokyo

PRINTING PARK SHIOJIRI
1991 Nagano

FUTAKOTAMAGAWA REDEVELOPMENT
1990 - 2001 Tokyo

TSUKIJI TEN HAUS
1990 - 1991 Tokyo

YAMANAKAKO PLATEAU COTTAGE
1991 - 1992 Yamanashi

SCOLA DE BELETZA
1991 Tokyo

TAKEUCHI RESIDENCE
1991 - 1993 Saitama

MATSUBARA RESIDENCE
1991 - 1993 Tokyo

LANDSCAPE FOR BLACK SLIDE MANTRA
1992 Sapporo

YOGA PROMENADE
1992 - 1993 Tokyo

AKASAKA MITOKO BUILDING
1992 Tokyo

MEGURO AOBADAI PROJECT
1992 - 1994 Tokyo

SHIMURA RESIDENCE
1992 - 1995 Tokyo

AMINO RESIDENCE
1992 - 1993 Tokyo

CHIBA MONORAIL STATION
1992 - 1998 Chiba

ARAKAWA RIVERFRONT FUTURE
VISION PROPOSAL
1992 - 1994 Tokyo

DEW MUSEUM
1993 - 1998 Tokyo
Associate: Nomura Co.,Ltd

MIKURIYA RESIDENCE
1993 - 1994 Tokyo

YANBA DAM 5 BRIDGES DESIGN
PROPOSAL
1993 Gunma
Associate: Construction Environmental Inst.

TOCHIGI SOFT RESEARCH PARK
1993 Tochigi

SANNOHE TOWN HALL
1993 - 1996 Aomori

SYSTEM SOLUTION CENTER TOCHIGI
1993 - 1995 Tochigi

TAKARAZUKA PROJECT
1993 Hyogo

ARAKAWA PEIL
1993 - 1994 Tokyo

IZU TEDDY BEAR MUSEUM
1993 - 1995 Shizuoka

TOTTORI FLOWER PARK
1993 - 1998 Tottori

WATANABE COTTAGE
1993 - 1994 Shizuoka

HAYASHI RESIDENCE
1993 - 1994 Tokyo

DR. SHIKATA RESIDENCE
1993 - 1995 Chiba

MINAMI IBARAKI TENNO HOUSING
1994 - 1998 Osaka

MORITA HEATDQUATERS BUILDING
1994 - 1995 Aichi

NAGANUMA ROAD SIDE STATION
1994 - 1996 Hokkaido

GASSAN TECHNO COMPLEX
1994 Korea

MESSAGE DE ROSE
1995 Tokyo

EKODA HOUSING
1995 Kanagawa

SAITAMA KANGO FUKUSHI COLLEGE PROJECT
1995 Saitama

HAMANAKO LANDSCAPE PROJECT
1995 Sizuoka

ENVIRONMENTAL SCIENCE CENTER
1995 Saitama

KONOSU CULTURAL CENTER
1996 Saitama

ARAKAWA RIVERFRONT FUTURE VISION PROPOSAL
1995 - 1996 Saitama

UCHIDA RESIDENCE
1995 Tokyo

SAKAMOTO RESIDENCE
1995 - 1996 Tokyo

SIRAKAMIYAMA VISITOR CENTER
1996 Aomori

BEN MEMORIAL RESEARCH CENTER
1994-1996 Tokyo

STUDIO ARCHITECT FIVE
1996 Tokyo

THE NOMURA SECURITES COTTAGE
1996 - 1997 Karuizawa

BELLE SIESTE
1996- 1997 Tokyo

NASU TEDDY BEAR MUSEUM
1996 - 1997 Tochigi

HOSOI OGIWARA RESIDENCE
1996 - 1997 Tokyo

TOYOTA RESORT PROJECT
1996 - 1997 Aichi

OBIRIN GAKUEN FUCHINOBE PROJECT
1998 Tokyo

SONY MUSIC ENTERTAINMENT SHIROGANEDAI OFFICE
1994 - 1998 Tokyo

MORITA COTTAGE
1997 - 1998 Karuizawa

KOMIYAMA PRINTING FACTORY
1997 - 1998 Saitama

SEKIGUCHI DOLL GARDEN
1997 - 1998 Sizuoka

ROOT HIGASHI UENO OFFICE
1996 - 1999 Tokyo

K-1 IIKURA HOTEL
1997 Tokyo

HAKONE TEDDY BEAR MUSEUM
1998- 1999 Hakone

MORINAGA CREATIVE LAB.
1999 Yokohama

MESSAGE DE ROSE VENUS FORT
1999 Tokyo

EXHIBITIONS

1987 "Design and Architecture"
100th Anniversary of the Tokyo Univ.
of Fine Arts

1990 "Last Decade"
Japan Design Comittee

1991~1994
"A/E/C System" Delphi Laboratory and JIA

1993 "Tradition and Today"
Tokyo Society of Architects & Building
Engineers

1994 "GA JAPAN LEAGUE '94"
GA Gallery

1994 "Architect 5 Partnership"
Japan Architects Club

1994 "Living Design Museum"
Living Design Center Ozone

1995 "Toward the New Possibility
of an Opening"
Japan Architects Club

1996 "Housing Exhibition" JIA

AWARDS

1989 Nikkei New Office Award
Ministry of Trade and Industry Award

1989 Sapporo Urban Landscape Award

1991 Japan Society of Architects Award

1994 Japan Townscape Award

1994 Railroad Architecture Award

1996 Nagoya Urban Landscape Award

1996 Nikkei New Office Award

1997 Tochigi Architecture Award

1997 Ministry of Trade and Industry
Good Design Award

1998 Saitama Landscape Award

1998 AACA Award

1999 Tokyo Architectural Award

1999 Chiba Architectural Culture Award

1991,1993,1996,1997,1998
Selected Architectural Designs of the AIJ

Partners

Junichi Kawamura JIA

1948
Born in Tokyo

1972
Tokyo Univ. of Fine Arts,
Department of Architecture BA

1974 Tokyo Univ. of Fine Arts,
Department of Architecture MA

1974
Kenzo Tange and URTEC

1982
Principal Architect

1986
Established ARCHITECT 5 PARTNERSHIP
Partner, CEO

1999
Advisor at the Isamu Noguchi Foundation of
Japan

Hidetsugu Horikoshi JIA

1953
Born in Tokyo

1976
Tokyo Univ. of Fine Arts, Department of
Architecture BA
(Ataka Award, Salon du Printemps Award)

1978
Tokyo Univ. of Fine Arts, Department of
Architecture MA

1978
Kenzo Tange and URTEC

1984
Principal Architect

1986
Established ARCHITECT 5 PARTNERSHIP
Partner, CEO

1997
Lecturer at the Nagoya Institute of Technology

Takeo Matsuoka JIA

1952
Born in Hyogo, brought up in Hokkaido

1976
Tokyo Univ. of Fine Arts,
Department of Architecture BA

1978
Tokyo Univ. of Fine Arts,
Department of Architecture MA

1978
Kenzo Tange and URTEC

1984
Principal Architect

1986
Established ARCHITECT 5 PARTNERSHIP
Partner, CEO

1999
Associate Professor at the Univ. of Shiga
Prefecture

Hirotaka Kidosaki JIA,SIA

1942
Born in Tokyo

1966
Nihon Univ. Faculty of Architecture BA

1966
Matsuda Hirata Architects and Planners

1977
Sheffield Univ. Faculty of Urban Planning MA

1979
Kenzo Tange and URTEC

1983
Registered Architect of SIA

1986
Executive Vice President

1993
Joined ARCHITECT 5 PARTNERSHIP
Partner, CEO

Staff

Minoru Nakao, Takahiro Terasawa,
Iwao Takeuchi, Kenji Itose,
Tadashi Shimizu, Tomonori Ookami,
Yuka Toyama, Tomohiro Morimoto,
Tomoko Yakuyama, Hiroaki Kamazawa,
Maki Kuratani, Kazuhiro Kitajima,

Ex-Associates & Staff

Tetsuo Furuichi, Nariaki Kato,
Michiyo Ikuno, Takeshi Araki,
Noboru Hasegawa, Hironori Mizoguchi,
Yasuhito Arasawa, Nobuko Kobayashi,
Yukiko Hatakeyama, Nobuyuki Nagahama,
Takemi Sato, Junko Suetake,
Koichi Inomata, Yumiko Yoneyama,
Keiko Mori, Shinya Hanazawa,
Kyoko Suwa, Yoko Aoki,
Yuichi Nagata, Hidetoshi Matsumoto,
Eiji Takashima, Terumasa Sato,
Takehiro Nakaya, Hiroko Takahashi,
Mitsuko Matsumoto, Shibuki Komatsu,
Hiroko Okamura, Akihiko Chiba,
Makoto Suzuki, Masao Yonemura

Architect 5 Partnership
http://www.architect5.co.jp